Play Piano!

a first book for beginners of all ages

Simon Henry

editor **Shona Grimbly**

ISBN 1 84044 115 1

Produced by:
The Brown Reference Group
8 Chapel Place
Rivington Street
London EC2A 3DQ, UK
www.brownreference.com

Editor: Shona Grimbly
Designer: Stefan Morris
Editorial Director: Lindsey Lowe
Managing Editor: Tim Cooke
Art Director: Dave Goodman
Production Manager: Alastair Gourlay

Printed and bound in China

contents

The keyboard   page **4**
How to sit at the keyboard
The keyboard pattern
Naming and finding the C key
Playing a pulse

Counting the beats   page **6**
Written music
Rhythm
Playing C and keeping the beat

Reading notes on the stave   page **8**
Treble and bass clefs
Reading and playing music

The minim note and rest   page **10**
Rhythm exercises using the crotchet and minim
Playing with minims

Time signatures   page **12**
March time
Playing in different time signatures

Using the fourth and fifth fingers   page **14**

Playing with two hands together   page **16**

Playing chords and the semibreve   page **18**
The semibreve and semibreve rest

Changing hand positions   page **20**

Tied and dotted notes   page **22**

Thumb under and C major scale   page **24**
Playing scales

Phrase marks and playing legato   page **26**
Playing loudly and softly

Making up your own tunes   page **28**
Using a ground bass

Building a repertoire   page **30**

Tunes to play
Chant   17
Empty streets   18
Ballad   19
Woodland stroll   21
Pachelbel's canon   21
Plain chant   22
"New world"   23
A short climb   25
Lilting melody   26
Reaching the summit   27
Oh when the saints   30
Jingle bells   31

the **keyboard**

how to sit at the **keyboard**

Sit slightly forward on your stool or chair, so your weight travels in a straight line from the top of your head through your back to your "tail."

Let your arms hang by your sides with the palms facing inward. Now bend your elbows so that your hands are in front of you. Your palms should face each other as if holding a large ball.

Rotate your hands so your palms are facing the floor. Your fingers should be slightly curved.

Let your fingers rest lightly on the piano keys. If necessary adjust the height and position of your chair so that the underside of your wrist, forearm and elbow form a straight line with the tips of your fingers. You are now sitting in the correct playing position.

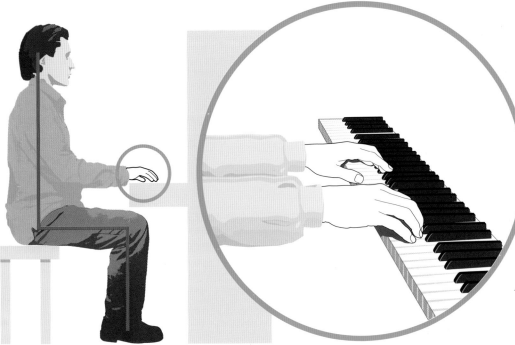

The correct sitting position

The position of the arm and hand

the piano

The full name of the piano is the "pianoforte," which comes from two Italian words meaning soft (*piano*) and loud (*forte*). It was named the pianoforte when it was invented in the 18th century because it could be played softly or loudly, unlike most earlier keyboard instruments, which did not permit the volume of sound to be varied.

fewer keys?

If you have an electronic keyboard you may find that it is shorter than the one shown here. Don't worry—only advanced players need to play the keys at the extreme ends of the full-size keyboard.

the **keyboard pattern**

Look carefully at your keyboard. You will see that the black keys and white keys are arranged in a regular pattern—groups of two and three black keys to each set of seven white keys. This means there is a pattern of five black keys and seven white keys that repeats along the length of the keyboard.

In a full-size keyboard (above) the pattern is repeated seven times with three extra keys at the lefthand end and one extra key at the right. There are 88 keys in all.

naming and finding the **C key**

Each key has a name. The white keys and the sounds they make are named using the first seven letters of the alphabet. The letter names are repeated for each pattern of seven white keys.

Look at the picture on the right. It shows part of a keyboard with the seven keys named, starting with C.

To find C on your keyboard, look for the white key immediately to the left of a pair of black keys. Then close your eyes and find it by touch. Now find all the Cs on your keyboard. How many are there?

Practise finding these C keys without looking at the keyboard, using either hand.

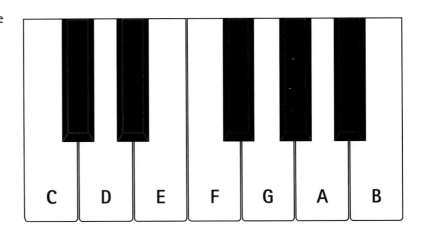

C D E F G A B

playing a **pulse**

Almost all music has a pulse, or regular repeated beat, that can be felt or heard. The pulse may be quite gentle or there may be an instrument, such as a drum, that plays a steady repeated beat throughout the music.

Practice clapping a steady pulse—not too fast. Imagine you are clapping in time with the ticking of a clock. Now you are ready to play a pulse at the keyboard.

Sit opposite the middle of your keyboard. Place the third finger of your right hand on any white key, halfway between the front edge and the line of black keys. Make sure your fingers are slightly curved so that the soft part of your finger tip is just touching the key.

Now press the key right down, gently but firmly. Lift your finger back to the starting position and repeat the action to create a regular pulse.

Repeat this exercise with your left hand. Then use other fingers to play white and black keys at various parts of the keyboard.

which finger?

To help you with your playing, music often suggests which finger to use. For this, your thumb is "1," your index finger is "2," the middle finger "3," the ring finger is "4," and the little finger is "5."

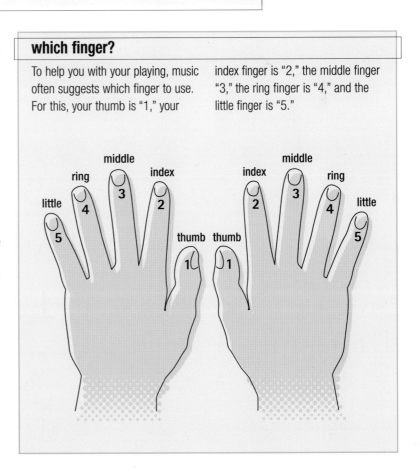

counting **the beats**

When you clap a pulse you are marking out the time with your beats like the ticking of a clock. We use this sense of a beat to organize musical sounds in time. By counting the beats we know when to play or stop playing.

Sit facing the middle of the keyboard and with your right thumb find the "middle" C by touch. Start by playing a regular pulse on C. Now play seven Cs and leave the eighth beat silent. Make sure the silence is one beat long. As you play, count the beats steadily up to eight.

Without looking down, find the white key to the right of C using your second finger. Again, play seven notes with the eighth beat silent. Do the same with your third finger on the next white key, your fourth finger on the next and your little finger on the next.

Go through the same steps with your left hand. Start with your thumb on C and then play each white key to the left of C with the next finger until you have played five different white keys.

music **terms**

Tempo is the musical word for the speed of the beat. When you are playing always try to keep a constant tempo.

Pitch is how high or low a note sounds. The pitch of each note is lower as you move down the keyboard to the left. As you move up the keyboard to the right, the pitch goes up.

written **music**

Written music tells you which keys to play, and how fast and for how long. It does this using notes, which are marks on the page like the ones shown here on the right.

This type of note is called a crotchet or quarter note. It lasts for one beat, and is played neither very fast nor very slow.

We can use crotchets to give us a steady pulse—imagine the beat of the footsteps of someone walking. When we want to count beats, we will use crotchets as our main unit of measure.

When we want silence lasting one beat we use a crotchet rest, shown here on the right.

So the exercise you just played in counting the beats, above, with seven notes and one beat silence looks like this:

the **crotchet**

The crotchet note is a filled-in round or oval shape with a stem attached to one side. It makes no difference to the sound if the stem points up or down, but the stem should go up if on the right of the note, and down if on the left.

rhythm

A rhythm is a pattern of beats and rests. Try clapping slowly the rhythm shown below. Tap with your foot to give you a regular pulse and clap the rhythm with your hands. Miss out a clap where you see a rest.

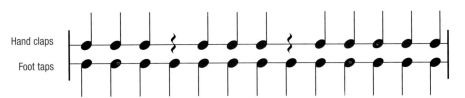

Now try tapping out the rhythm below using both hands. Sit at a table and tap the upper part with your right hand, at the same time tapping the lower part with your left hand. Make sure both hands keep together, tapping a regular beat. Miss out a tap for each rest.

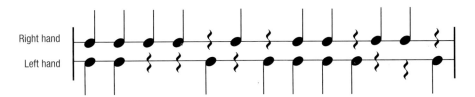

playing C and keeping the beat

You are now ready to transfer your rhythm skills to the keyboard. Find C on your keyboard and play the first two patterns on the right first with your right thumb and then with your left. Then play the third pattern with the right and left thumbs as shown. Make sure you count aloud as you play, keeping a regular pulse.

Notice the vertical lines on the exercises. These are called bar lines, and they are used to divide music up into sections. This makes it easier for the player to keep track of the notes. It also means we only need count the small number of beats between bar lines and then repeat.

Although bar lines divide the music up they do not interrupt the flow.

The space between bar lines is called a bar or measure. In these exercises there are four beats in each bar.

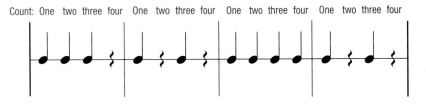

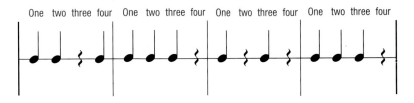

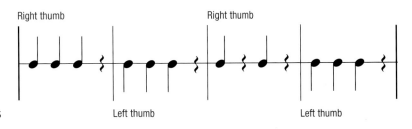

As well as telling you about rhythm, written notes tell you which keys to play.

Notes are written on five lines, called a stave. We read music from left to right, just as we read words in a book. Here are some notes written on a stave:

You can see that some notes are written in the spaces between the lines, and some are written across the lines, with half the note above the line and half below.

As we go up the stave, the notes sound higher. As we go down the stave, the notes sound lower. If you were to sing the example above,

you would sing four notes, each sounding slightly higher than the one before, then your voice would have to make a bigger jump up to a high note, followed by a jump down to a note that is lower than the first note.

You can think of the stave as a series of steps. Look at the stave below and you will see that the five lines plus four spaces give us nine steps.

When you sit at the piano the notes to your right sound higher than the notes to your left. So when you climb up the steps of the stave, your fingers will travel from left to right along the keyboard.

treble and **bass clefs**

the clefs

The first clefs were letter forms that showed how the letter names given to the keys on the keyboard matched up to the notes written on the stave. The treble clef was a G written on the second line up, showing that the note written on this line was G. In the bass clef the letter F was written on the second line down, showing that the note written on this line was F. Over the years the letters G and F took on the stylized form used today.

Look at the two staves below. At the start of each stave (at the lefthand edge) there is a special mark. These marks are called clefs.

The first clef is called the treble clef. It tells us that the notes written on this stave will be the higher notes, generally those above (to the right of) the middle of the keyboard. The notes in the treble clef are normally played with the right hand by keyboard players.

The clef on the lower stave is called the bass clef. It tells us that the notes on this stave will be the lower notes of the keyboard, generally those below (on the left of) the middle. These notes are normally played with the left hand.

Notice that there is one note floating between the two staves. It has its own short line to sit across. This note is called Middle C.

The little line Middle C sits across is called a ledger line. It is as if there were an 11th line missing between the two staves. Middle C can "belong" to either the treble or the bass clef.

On either side of Middle C are the notes B and D. B sits on the top line of the stave in the bass clef. D sits just under the bottom line of the stave in the treble clef. They are like notes in spaces, although B does not actually have a line above it, and D does not have a line below it.

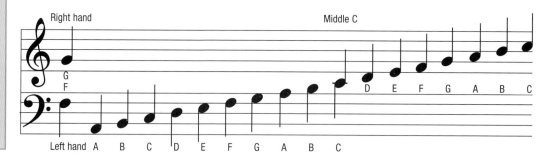

remembering the names of the notes on the stave

Here are some ways to help you remember the names of the notes on the staves.

In the **treble** clef the notes in the spaces spell FACE. The notes on the lines stand for Every Green Bus Drives Fast. The notes in the spaces of the **bass** clef stand for Armadillos Can Easily Grow. The notes on the lines stand for Good Boys Deserve Fish and Chips.

Or you can make up your own nonsense sentences to help you remember the note names.

reading and playing music

You are now ready to start reading and playing music. On the right are the notes you have already played with each hand.

Now play the piece below. Keep your eyes on the music and trust your hands and ears to tell you that you are playing the correct notes.

Play with a slow, steady beat, paying particular attention to the crotchet rests. To help you we have shown on the music which finger you should use for each note.

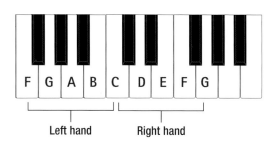

Left hand   Right hand

Practice piece: **Up to D and down to B**

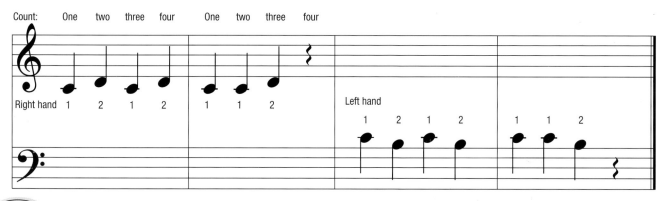

the **minim note** and **rest**

So far you have used crotchets and crotchet rests, which are each worth one beat. Now you will start to use minims (also called half notes) and minim rests. They are shown on the right. They are each worth two beats, so they last twice as long as crotchets.

The minim rest is a small filled-in rectangle that sits on the middle line of the stave.

You can see that the note head of the minim is not filled in. It has a stem like a crotchet—the stem usually points down for notes above the middle line of the stave and up for notes below the middle line.

the **end**

We add an extra thick bar line to show where the music ends. It acts like a full stop.

The stems of notes written on the middle line of the stave can point either up or down.

rhythm exercises using **the crotchet** and **minim**

Here are two rhythm exercises to tap out to get you used to the minim. Tap the top line with your right hand and the bottom line with your left. The tap for the minim tells you where the note starts rather than where it finishes.

Tap each exercise through four times, until you are accustomed to the idea of tapping or playing two crotchets to one minim.

Remember not to tap where you see a rest sign.

10

playing with **minims**

Here are some pieces to play using minims. In the first piece the right hand plays C and D, and the left hand plays C and B. Remember to count the beats out loud as you play. There are four beats in each bar.

Practice piece: **Two notes for each hand**

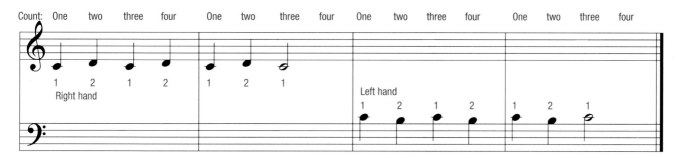

In the next two pieces the right hand plays C, D and E while the left hand plays C, B and A.

Practice piece: **Three notes each**

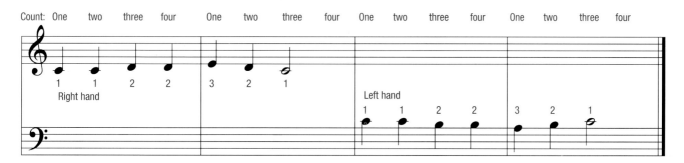

Practice piece: **Thinking minims**

time signatures

Most music, particularly music such as dance music, gives us a sense of a pulse running through it. Also, most music gives us the feeling that some beats are stronger than others, that is, they are accented.

In some music it is the first of every two beats that feels stronger. In other pieces it is the first of every three beats, and in others the first of every four beats is accented.

For example, when people are marching, the beat when they move their left foot might be accented. This would mean accenting the first of every two beats as in the example shown below. The sign > means the beat is accented.

Listen to different pieces of music and clap the pulse—the regular beat—that fits the music. Clap louder on the beat that feels stronger. Is it the first of two, three or four beats?

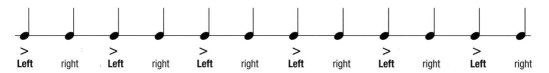

march time

Below we show you how the beat for a march tune is written. Instead of marking the accented notes, bar lines are used to show how the beats are grouped. A time signature at the beginning tells us how many beats, and what kind of beats, there are in each bar.

Because the music is for marching, each bar is worth two beats. The top number of the time signature tells us how many beats there are in each bar—two in this case. The bottom number tells us what kind of beat—in this case each beat is worth a crotchet, or quarter note.

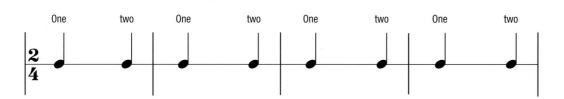

Practice piece: **An obvious march**

Here is a march tune for you to play. Accent the first note in each bar so that you get a strong feeling of "**one**, two, **one**, two," or "**left**, right, **left**, right."

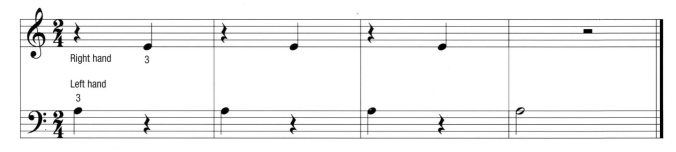

SING "Left   right,   left,   right,   then   stand   still"

playing in different time signatures

The time signatures you will meet most often will be 2:4, 3:4 and 4:4. That is, music with two crotchet beats, three crotchet beats or four crochet beats in each bar.

Practice clapping the time signatures of the pieces below. Clap loudly on the first beat in each bar and softly on the other beats.

Now play these pieces. They all have different time signatures. Count the beats steadily as you play.

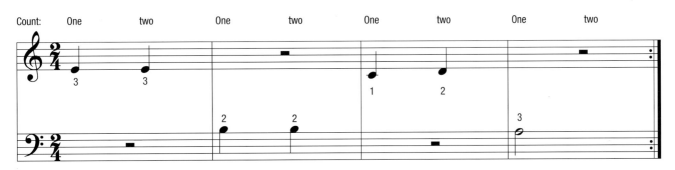

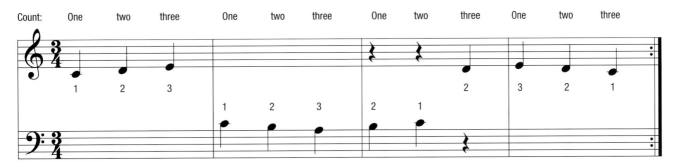

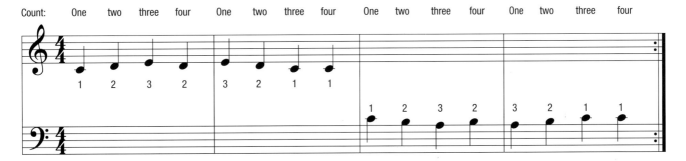

the waltz

The waltz was a dance that became very popular in Vienna at the end of the 18th century. It was danced to music in 3:4 time. A well known waltz tune is "The Blue Danube."

repeat marks

You will notice that in the pieces above there are some special marks at the end. A pair of dots before the thin and thick lines means "repeat," that is, go back to the beginning and play the music again.

using the **fourth** and **fifth fingers**

So far the pieces you have played have used just three fingers of each hand. Now you will start to use the fourth and fifth fingers.

These fingers are generally thought to be the weaker fingers. So play these exercises regularly to give them plenty of practice.

Practice piece: **Steps**

Practice piece: **Four for each hand**

The following exercises are for all five fingers of each hand. Using the fifth finger extends your range of notes in the right hand to G, and in your left hand to F. Look at the time signature before you start to play, and count the beats in each bar.

fingerings

Written music will usually give you some indication of which fingers to use to play the notes. Where the fingering is not written on the music it is either obvious, or the same as given earlier, or up to you to choose.

Practice piece: **More steps**

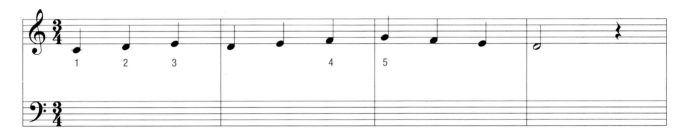

In the next piece you will find that your fingers are not always playing in steps. To help you the recommended fingering is written by each note.

Practice piece: **Five fingers each**

15

playing with **two hands** together

You have already played several pieces using the right and left hands separately. Now it is time to play with both hands together.

Look at the piece below, which is in 4:4 time (four beats to the bar). Start by playing each hand separately, counting the beats carefully.

When you are ready, play the piece as written, that is, with your two hands together. Have the thumb of your left hand ready to start playing at the beginning of the second bar.

Practice piece: **Duet**

The next piece is not as difficult as it looks because for the first three bars the notes in both hands move up and down together. Again, play each hand separately, counting the beats, before you try to play the hands together.

Note that in the left hand the second finger plays C. This means that the thumb can play D—the note just above C—which is written on the ledger line.

Practice piece: **Parallel lines**

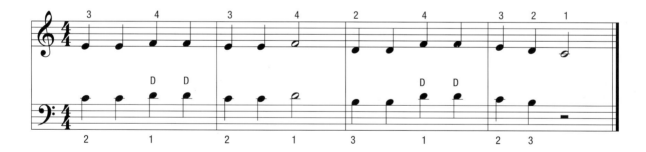

the **note D**

In the piece "Parallel lines" the note D above Middle C is written in two ways, depending on which hand is playing it. In the treble clef it hangs just below the bottom line of the stave. In the bass clef it sits on the ledger line just above Middle C.

Look at the music for the next piece carefully before you start practising it. You will see that in the first and third lines the right hand only plays one note—F. In the second and fourth lines the left hand only plays two notes—A and G. If you are aware of this you will find it easier to concentrate on the notes in the other hand.

The right hand starts with the fourth finger on E, which allows you to play the B in the second line with your thumb. The B is written just below the ledger line that Middle C is written on. In the left hand, B is written sitting on the top line of the bass clef stave. Play each hand separately first, before playing hands together.

A tune to play: **Chant**

ritardando

music **terms**

Ritardando means "gradually slowing down." Where you see this written on the music you should gradually reduce the tempo.

playing **chords** and the **semibreve**

A chord is two or more notes played at the same time. Here are some simple, two-note chords for both the right and left hands. Play them using the fingering shown.

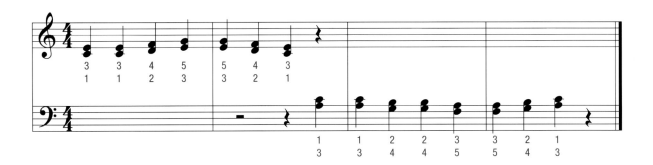

Now try playing this tune. Practise the left hand on its own first, until you are quite sure of the chords.

A tune to play: **Empty streets**

the **semibreve** and **semibreve rest**

So far you have only used two kinds of note—the crotchet and the minim. Now you are going to start playing music with a new note called the semibreve, or whole note.

The semibreve lasts for four beats, as does the semibreve or whole note rest. They are shown on the right. The semibreve note is not filled in and has no stem. The semibreve rest hangs from the second line down on the stave.

Practise tapping this rhythm exercise, giving one beat to each crotchet, two beats to each minim, and four beats to each semibreve.

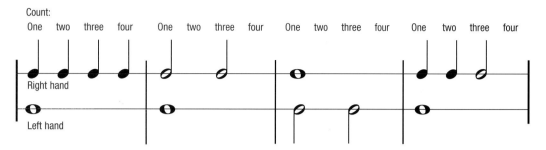

Now play this practice piece, counting the beats carefully. Make sure you hold the semibreves for the full count of four.

A tune to play: **Ballad**

changing **hand positions**

So far most of the pieces you have played have been performed with your hands in the same "starting position." This position is with the right and left thumbs playing Middle C.

Sometimes you will start a piece with your hands in a different place on the keyboard. Or you may need to change your hand position on the keyboard in the middle of a piece to enable you to play higher or lower notes.

If you start with your right thumb on F in the treble clef, for example, you will be able to play up to the C above Middle C. And starting with your left thumb on F in the bass clef will enable you to play the five notes below F.

Play the exercise below, starting with your right thumb on F in the treble clef and your left thumb on F in the bass clef. You can now play A and C in the treble clef, and E in the bass.

Practice piece: **Starting on F**

Now move both your thumbs onto the Gs and play this exercise. Starting on G means you can now play up to D in the treble clef and down to C in the bass clef.

Practice piece: **Thumbs on G**

are you **sitting** comfortably?

Remember to check your sitting position every time you sit at the keyboard. Your back should be straight, and the tips of your fingers and the underside of your wrist and forearm should also be in a straight line. Adjust the height and position of your chair if necessary so that you are sitting in the correct position.

Here are two tunes that use new hand positions. Follow the fingering carefully to play a whole new range of notes.

"Woodland stroll" starts with your right third finger on B and your left fifth finger on G.

In "Pachelbel's canon" you will find that your right hand has to "jump" to a different position at the beginning of several bars to play A and G. These notes follow on below Middle C and B and need a second ledger line. The left hand changes position to play the large steps.

A tune to play: **Woodland stroll**

A tune to play: **Pachelbel's canon**

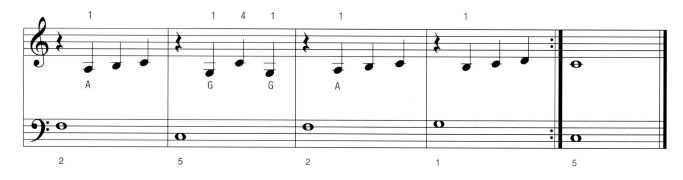

tied and dotted notes

tied notes

Sometimes in written music you will see two notes of the same pitch joined by a slightly curved line. The curved line is called a "tie." When two notes are tied together like this the second note is not played as a separate note. You simply hold onto the first note for the additional beats.

So when a minim is tied to a crotchet, you hold the note for three beats.

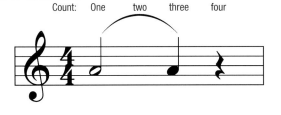

Now play "Plain chant" fairly slowly, holding the tied notes for three beats.

A tune to play: **Plain chant**

dotted notes

When a dot is placed after a note it makes the note length half as long again. So a dot placed after a minim means the note will last for three beats (2 + 1 = 3). A dot can be placed after any note—it will add on half the time value of the note.

A minim with a dot after it is called a "dotted minim." Play these pieces, holding the dotted minims for three beats. In "New world" you will need to stretch the fingers of your left hand wider than usual to play some of the chords.

Practice piece: **Dotted minims**

A tune to play: **"New world"**

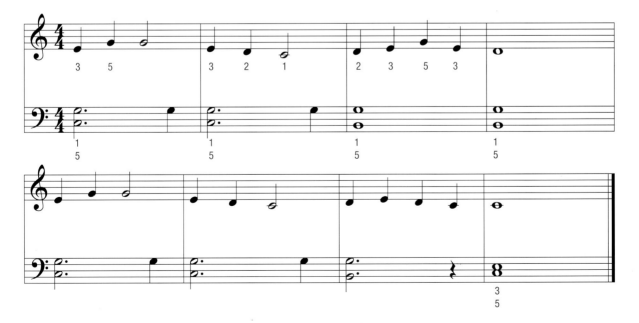

23

thumb under and C major scale

Most of the pieces you have played so far have used only five notes in each hand. What do you do if you want to play a run of notes like the one shown on the right, where there are more than five notes going up in steps?

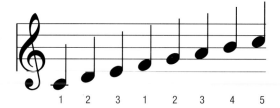

This is what you do. Play the first three notes with the thumb, second and third fingers of your right hand. Then, while your third finger is on the E, bring your thumb **under** your other fingers and place it on the F. As you do this lift your third finger off the E and move your hand into a normal playing position—with your thumb now starting on F. You can now carry on playing up to C.

Practise doing this several times. Then practise coming down, reversing the playing order

shown above. When you get to F bring your third finger **over** your thumb to play the E, then carry on down to the C. Also practise with the left hand, starting with your thumb on Middle C. As the left hand moves down the keyboard, the thumb will pass under the third finger to play G, and enable you to carry on to lower C.

This technique is called "thumb under" and "third finger over," and is used by pianists to enable them to play a long run of notes.

playing **scales**

When notes are arranged in order of pitch, going from a low note to a high note of the same name, the pattern of notes is called a scale. When we play scales, we finish on the same note name that we started on, and we name the scale after the starting note. There are various types of scale. Each type of scale sounds different and has its own character and creates its own mood. The one shown below is called the "C major" scale.

Play this scale of C major with the right hand first, using the thumb under technique that you practised above. When you play down the scale, your third finger passes over your thumb.

Then play the scale with your left hand. Start on finger 5 and play up to G, when your third finger passes over the thumb to carry on up to Middle C. Coming down your thumb passes under your third finger to complete the scale.

Practice piece: **Scale of C major**

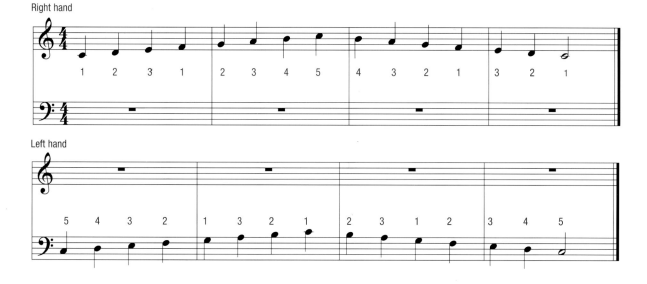

Now you can try playing the scale with both hands together in "contrary motion." This is easier than it looks, because both hands do thumb under at the same time.

Practice piece: **Contrary motion**

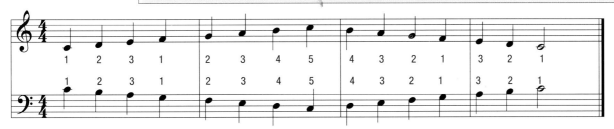

When you feel confident playing in contrary motion, you can try playing the scale in "similar motion." This is slightly more difficult as the thumbs move at different times, although both third fingers are played together.

Practice piece: **Similar motion**

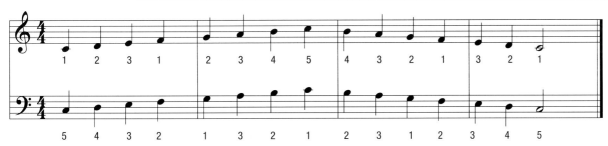

Now play this tune, which uses the thumb under technique in the right hand.

A tune to play: **A short climb**

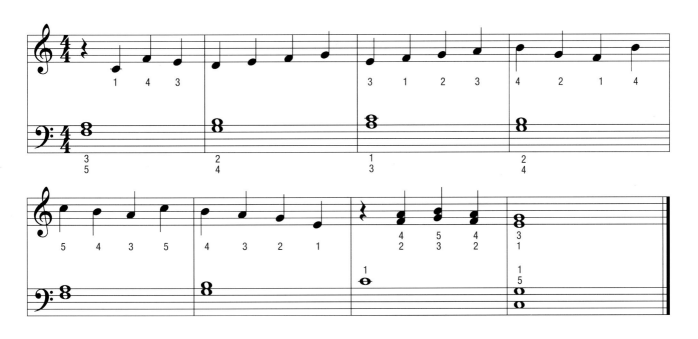

phrase marks and playing legato

Imagine you are singing a tune without words. You can either sing each note as "tah" or as "ah." If you sing the notes as "tah" the tune will sound like "tah-tah-tah-tah." Each note will be slightly detached from the next. But if you sing "ah" the notes will flow together like this "aaaaaaah."

When you play from written music the first sort of sound is what you would aim for if you just saw a row of notes. But if you see a curved line above or below a run of notes (as in "Lilting melody" below) you should aim for the second effect, making the notes run together.

This is called "legato" and means the notes should be played smoothly with no break between them.

The curved line is called a slur, or phrase mark.

Now play this piece. Where you see a phrase mark connecting the notes, try to move from one note to the next without any break in the sound.

A tune to play: **Lilting melody**

playing **loudly** and **softly**

One of the special features of the piano when it was invented was that it could be played loudly or softly. You can play loudly on the piano by playing the keys with more weight than usual, and softly by using a more gentle touch.

Special instructions called dynamics are put on music to tell you whether to play loudly or softly. Loudly is indicated by an "*f*," standing for *forte*, the Italian word for "strong." Softly is indicated by "*p*," standing for the Italian word *piano*, meaning "soft." So "*pp*" means very softly and "*mp*" ("*mezzo piano*") "half soft."

Similarly "*mf*" ("*mezzo forte*") means "half loud" or not as loud as "*f*."

The piece "Reaching the summit" below can be played quite slowly. Notice the tied notes in the first line, which are held over to the next bar.

The piece begins very softly ("*pp*") and gradually builds up in volume to "*f*" (loud).

Pay careful attention to the instructions *pp*, *mp*, *mf* and *f* when they appear and play each section louder than the previous one to achieve the desired effect.

A tune to play: **Reaching the summit**

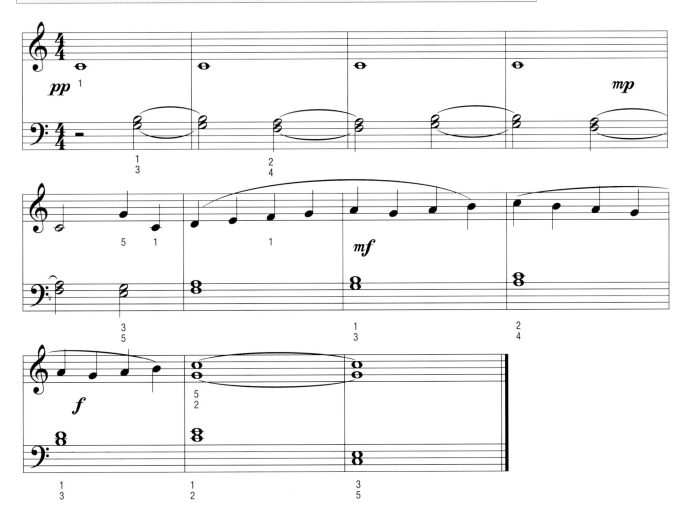

making up **your own tunes**

Music is often written down, or "composed," by one person and then performed by other people at another time and place. Some music, however, is made up at the time of performance, or "improvised." Jazz and classical Indian music are two traditions in which improvisation plays an important role.

You do not have to be an experienced musician to try improvising. It can be fun just to experiment on the keyboard and see what happens. Here are some stepping stones to get you started.

Try playing the phrase of music in the first two bars of these pieces and then, without stopping to think, play your own "answering phrase" to complete the four bars.

Two bars given and two for you

1   3   4   4   3

1   3   4   2   3

4   5   3   4   3   2   2   1

3   1   3   1   5   5   5

3   4   5   3   4   5

using a **ground bass**

Another useful technique for improvising your own tunes is to use four bars of a bass part in the left hand that you repeat over and over again while you play your own improvised tune in the right hand.

You could start with a very simple bass line like this:

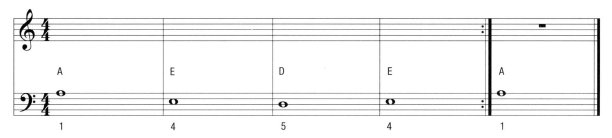

And perhaps start off in the right hand like this:

You can continue improvising in the right hand while the left hand repeats the bass line as long as you wish. When a bass line is used like this throughout a piece, it is called a "ground bass."

Here is another bass line that you could go on repeating while you improvise over the top. You could also experiment using chords in the right hand as shown here.

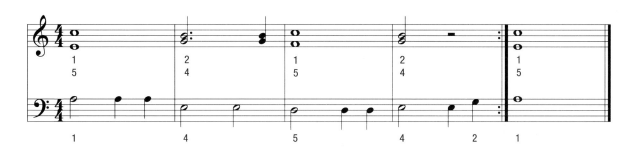

building **a repertoire**

Now that you can play confidently with both hands you will want to show off your new skills to family and friends. It is a good idea to have a collection of favourite pieces that you practise regularly so that you always have something ready to play. Here are two familiar tunes to start your repertoire.

A tune to play: **Oh when the saints**

In this piece your lefthand fingers will have to
stretch wide to play some of the chords.

A tune to play: **Jingle bells**

notepad

Below is a page of music staves on which you can practise writing notes, rests, and treble and bass clefs. You can also use it for writing down your first improvised tunes.

Diving Doodlebugs.